5 DAYS OF A

GRAND PRIX

Other books by Macmillan

DAMON HILL'S GRAND PRIX YEAR

POLE POSITION

INSIDE FORMULA ONE

AGAINST THE ODDS
JORDAN'S DRIVE TO WIN

5 DAYS OF A
GRAND PRIX

JON NICHOLSON & ADAM PARSONS

First published 1999 by Macmillan
an imprint of Macmillan Publishers Limited
25 Eccleston Place, London SW1W 9NF
Basingstoke and Oxford

Associated companies throughout the world

ISBN 0 333 74700 5

Text copyright © Adam Parsons 1999
Photographs copyright © Jon Nicholson 1999

1 3 5 7 9 8 6 4 2

A CIP catalogue record for this book is available
from the British Library.

Designed by Macmillan General Books Design Department.
Printed and bound in Italy by New Interlitho, Spa, Milan

'In the last five years or so I have been in the privileged position of witnessing my friend, Damon Hill, reach his lifelong dream of winning the FIA World Championship in 1996. In the melting pot of press speculation and rumour called the paddock, stirred occasionally by the powers that be, one becomes quite blasé about such things as which country one is in, or what restaraunt to eat in that night. But if some of these people ventured into the hills and crowds that surround a Grand Prix circuit they would find a breath of fresh air which would reinstall the passion of the grass-root fan, sleeping in the mud for four days, not caring about much else than watching a good clean motor race.

'I would like to thank all the teams who gave me a little bit of help and the Austrians who got me so full of beer and schnapps in Imola that I too found myself sleeping on the Rivazza hillside on Thursday afternoon.'

Jon Nicholson

'It took the combined efforts of two sports editors, Nick Pitt and Jeff Randall, to earn me a place in the motor-racing paddock, so I owe both of them a debt of gratitude for everything that has followed. Within Formula One, so many people, from drivers to mechanics, and journalists to team owners, have helped me that it would not be fair to name some and miss out others. Suffice to say that to all those who have offered me stories, interviews, coffee, sandwiches, spare batteries, lifts, last-minute quotes and friendship, I would like to say thanks.'

Adam Parsons

'Since graduating from university with a Masters Degree in Printing Theory, I have been applying my knowledge and printing methods as a photographer and professional printer.

'I joined Metro Art Department in March 1998 and had the opportunity to experiment with many conventional and historical printing processes.

'Working closely with photographers such as Jon, I prefer to have an open approach to printing and have no set rules, allowing me to be more sensitive to the individual subject matter.

'I admire Jon's individual style and approach to his work and I feel that the F1 series clearly underlines, as on past projects, his passion for photography.'

Steve Macleod

M E T R O
IMAGING

Introduction

An empty sports stadium is a desolate place in which to find yourself. Grandstands that once struggled to contain their excited crowds become empty and redundant after the fans have drifted away and the glow slowly dwindles from steeply looming floodlights. The cacophony that rumbles around any great occasion blows away on the wind, to be replaced by a whistling draught and the distant noise of congested ring roads. With a capacity crowd inside, Wembley Stadium or the San Siro in Milan are remarkable vistas of colour and passion, but close the doors at the end of a day and even the most famous arena seems little more than a cavernous concrete bowl.

People, rather than their surroundings, create the feelings of anticipation and joy that are summed up by a single, intangible word – 'atmosphere'. It is people who cheer and welcome, applaud and berate, and they who bring a sporting event to life with their enthusiasm. In a world without supporters professional sport would collapse, for its fortunes rise and fall in time with the fans. Without them it would be bankrupt in both income and purpose.

For football, it is the intimacy of the match that provides the link, the feeling of belonging that comes with being part of a swaying crowd. Similarly, an international rugby match or a Grand Slam tennis final would be nothing without the fans. Even snooker, that most calculating and distant of spectacles, needs its sense of humanity and occasion.

Motor racing, though, is subtly different because, with the pointed exception of the adoration that follows Ferrari around Italy, the sport does not have the tribal following of football, nor the ingrained nationalism of cricket or rugby. There are supporters, of course, fans who will paint their faces and wave a flag, but they do not have the same level of overt hysteria as their footballing counterparts. The sporting obsession is the same, but the symptoms and loyalties are markedly different.

Nationalism produces its own occasional waves, such as those that have seen both Nigel Mansell and Damon Hill transformed into British icons in recent years and Michael Schumacher all but deified in the minds of many Germans, but only in Italy, in the midst of the obsessive chorus of fans known as the *tifosi*, do the two sports find a common ground of devotion and blind optimism.

In Italy, motor racing does not have to compete with golf, tennis, cricket or rugby for the favoured position alongside football in the nation's affections. While Britain has always had a tradition of engineering excellence that bonds the country to Formula One, Italy has been able to wallow in the exuberance of Ferrari, Alfa Romeo, Lancia, Bugatti and Lamborghini, sports car manufacturers producing small numbers of vehicles that have the speed and agility to match their beauty. If motor racing is a cerebral sport to many of its followers, in Italy it is one of passion and instinct.

Even now, at a time when the world's roads are cluttered, the sight of a red Ferrari is enough to bring people to their feet in any country. It is a potent symbol of bravado, a treasure that has earned the admiration of the world and become a coat of arms for Italy's self-confidence. The red colour scheme provides the link to distant eras, and the name is recognized everywhere. Deep down in all of us is the desire to wake up one day with a Ferrari parked in the garage.

The reputation comes from the sporting heritage, from the toys and photographs that every child sees of red racing cars. True to that sense of history, Ferrari are now the only team left in Formula One to build both the chassis and the engine of their cars, a feat of engineering unparalleled in motorsport around the world.

Everybody else, including the latter-day luminaries at Williams and McLaren, build and design the car, but bring the engine in from an outside engineering company such as Mecachrome, Mugen or Ilmor, the British company that quietly builds the engines for Mercedes-Benz and allows the Germans to take the credit.

Ferrari, though, do the lot themselves, spending a great deal of money in the process. In 1998, Ferrari's budget to complete the Formula One season was estimated to be more than

£100 million, a figure far exceeding that of any other team and almost ten times the sum spent by the smallest, Minardi.

Their money comes largely from sponsors, including Marlboro and Shell, multinational names who pay small fortunes to associate themselves with the famous red cars. To them, it matters little that Ferrari have not won a drivers' championship since 1979, for the reputation of the team is based on the heart rather than the mind. However chronic their underachievement, the Ferrari name is still clearly the most evocative in Formula One, and its sponsors pay accordingly.

Like the famous sights of Monza or Silverstone, Ferrari's appeal lies in its ability to provide a tangible bridge between the sport's past and present. Enzo Ferrari founded the team in 1929 and spent the first decade racing cars built by Alfa Romeo. From 1938 onwards, though, Ferrari went his own way, and his team have followed that singular path ever since.

The list of drivers who have been employed by them reads like a roster of the great. Fangio, Ascari, Lauda, Collins, Villeneuve, Mansell, Prost and now Schumacher have all lit up the stage with their performances at the wheel of a red racing car, all of them enhancing the sweet romanticism that burns at the core of Formula One.

'When we test our cars, people who live nearby open their windows to hear,' said Ross Brawn, the considered Englishman who is now Ferrari's technical director. 'In England, they would be on the phone to the council to complain about the noise, but in Italy it is part of the history. They want to hear the Ferrari engine. To them, it's music.'

May motor racing never lose that soft heart, for it is a spectacle as much as a sport, a form of live entertainment with the same excitable lure as a fairground rollercoaster. More than any other sport, it puts on a spectacular show that leaves its audience hungry for more and then, like a travelling circus, it moves on to another city.

The circus analogy is peculiarly appropriate to Formula One. For most of its season, the sport carts its paraphernalia around Europe in a caravan of brightly painted lorries, transporting its cars and machinery from place to place. It has its own fairground, a swath of fiercely guarded tarmac known as the paddock where trucks are unloaded and cars prepared, and it has crowds of wide eyed punters, queuing up to spend their money on watching brave men pushing themselves to the limit. It even has a ringmaster, although the control held by Bernie Ecclestone, motor racing's impresario supreme, owes more to the power of the dollar than to the fear of any horsewhip.

It is a sport in transit, one with very few permanent offices to tie it down to a single home, yet, for all that restlessness, motor racing prizes its venues with more relish than any other sport. The names of the circuits have a resonance of their own, an ancestry that lends them individual characteristics. Some tracks are regarded as fearsome and approached in trepidation; others seem more friendly and approachable. They are the regular haunts of an itinerant circus. So they are its homes, and they are loved accordingly.

For most of the year the Silverstone racing circuit, Britain's motorsport hub, stands as stark and windswept as a moun-tainside, sending a freezing chill through those who visit it. It was once an airbase, and a well-placed one at that, for the view of green fields and undulating woodland extends for mile upon unbroken mile.

It has been decades since Air Force planes used Silverstone regularly, but it is a measure of Formula One's rampant commercialism that the annual arrival of grand prix cars returns the circuit in part to its airfield origins, a response to the corporate entertainment that forms a significant part of the sport's modern revenue. Companies pay many hundreds of pounds to entertain a single person for one day in the lavish ivy-draped suites that are put up for the occasion, and they want a return on such an investment.

With so much money being spent, those doing the entertaining have little desire to inflict traffic jams on their guests, so they bring them in by helicopter instead. As do the teams and some of the more well-heeled supporters, who fly into Silverstone in time for the start of the race and then soar home afterwards.

The sky fills with helicopters landing and then taking off once more to pick up the next load of commuters. Indeed, so relentless is the whirring of rotor blades that, on the morning of the British Grand Prix, Silverstone's small landing strip is the busiest airport in the world. Like that scene in *Apocalypse Now*, helicopters arrive in an endless stream, wheeling over the circuit to drop off their passengers and then disappearing again to pick up their next group. Somewhere in the heavens, there must be a Royal Air Force base commander who looks down at his old landing strip each July in utter bemusement.

It was Silverstone's origins that made it such an

appropriate place for motor racing after the end of the Second World War, with the runways being used as ad-hoc straights, just as they are at races in America today. In those early days, a pair of inward straights at either side of the circuit gave the impression that drivers were heading directly towards one another in a game of high-speed chicken, but the circuit has been heavily modified and rebuilt over the passing decades, its original design changed beyond recognition.

As a teenager, I sat in the Woodcote grandstand with my father and watched Keke Rosberg pass by on his way to the fastest lap in Formula One's history. In that single moment, Rosberg, a phlegmatic Finn who smoked heavily and drove his car like a rancher taming a wild steer, embodied the sport's pure dynamism. His car was sliding on a still-damp surface and he was evidently wrestling to keep it under control. One of the four wheels was off the ground as he stamped on the brakes and the rear of the car momentarily flicked sideways before the driver regained control with an instinctive violent jerk. Then he was gone, and the crowd sighed as one, a thousand spectators who had all been holding their breath suddenly finding the time to exhale. When he next came past, slowing to return to the pits, pole position safely secured, he received a standing ovation.

It is from such moments that motor racing's appeal is hewn, moments when its participants and their machinery are pushed to the extremes of endurance. Television coverage of the sport has taken broadcasting technology to new heights, but it struggles to bring home the sheer emotion that passes through the crowd like an electric current when it sees a sight as remarkable as Rosberg's screaming, sliding car.

Indeed, the advancing technology of motor racing's television camerawork has had the effect of smoothing the edges rather too much and giving Formula One the sanitized feel of a Hollywood movie. The pictures are so sharp and crisply edited that it is easy to forget that you are watching a live sporting event and instead imagine yourself sitting in a cinema, watching a careful piece of choreography. *Grand Prix*, the feature film made in 1966, certainly has a rawer edge to it than the broadcasts of today's races that are beamed around the world.

When you are there at the track, though, listening to the coarse sounds of the engines and seeing the drivers' helmets bobbing up and down in the cockpit, there is no mistaking the vitality of the sport. For those at home, it is an entertainment, but for the spectators who watch in person, motor racing remains the same exacting spectacle it has always been.

Silverstone, though, offers a different challenge for today's drivers, the emphasis having been transferred away from sheer bravery and towards technique and consistency. Even the days of Rosberg's flying lap seem long distant, for Silverstone's corners have tightened since then and speeds have dropped. Races are run to a maximum distance of 200 miles and cars doing 160mph per lap, and rising, were liable to produce grands prix that were completed in only an hour and a quarter; too short for comfort.

So Silverstone's circuit sprouted some new corners to slow down its racers and, while it was about it, the circuit also revived its commercial heart. These days, it bustles with junior races, driving schools and corporate events. It has the sort of smart front entrance that would win due approval of marketing people, a huge arch that announces itself with cheerful lettering, and there are permanent grandstands dotted all over the circuit, with souvenir stands lying in wait and refreshment huts that look like pampered garden sheds. The hospitality facilities installed over the past few years have cost millions of pounds, and the medical centre would be the envy of most hospitals.

But it is only for a few weekends each year that Silverstone's plastic seats are filled to their capacity. Touring car races draw decent crowds and so do the large GT machines that thunder round like charging elephants, but only once each season does the circuit really fill up and that, of course, is when the Formula One circus comes to town.

It doesn't seem to matter that the ticket prices are as high as the Goodyear blimp, nor that the traffic congestion has to be seen to be believed. Every year, the British Grand Prix is a sell-out and usually the tickets have all been snapped up several months in advance, including tens of thousands of general admission tickets that do not even guarantee a decent view of the track, but which cost nearly a hundred pounds. It is an outrageous price to place on a day's spectating but, as you leave Silverstone on a Saturday night, there are already queues of cheerful fans forming with just these sort of tickets, ready to rush in when the gates open a little after dawn and capture a few square feet of vantage point. If they are being ripped off, they don't appear to mind.

But why should rational people go to such painful lengths simply to watch cars going round in circles? The answer lies in that indefinable sense of atmosphere and in the pleasure of being present at a sporting event that is still steeped in unpredictability. The onset of rain can change races completely, and there is always the lurking risk of an accident, a careless mistake or a mechanical failure waiting to trip up a driver.

In the last race of the 1998 season, Michael Schumacher, the finest racing driver in the world, needed to win the Japanese Grand Prix to stand a chance of being champion for the third time. He qualified in pole position, looked confident before the race and then, to the astonishment of a watching world, stalled his engine on the starting grid. For all the excuses that were trotted out in his defence, it was 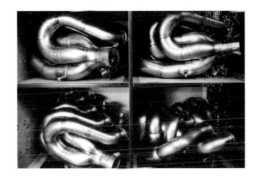 an error that defied simple explanation, one that took time to register in the observer's mind. In a single act, the strength of motor racing was typified; the totem brought back to earth by a freak, unpredictable event, the genius caught out. Schumacher's stationery Ferrari became a freeze-frame in the mind of all who saw it, just like Rosberg's sliding car thirteen years before.

It was another memory to add to the library that Formula One so cherishes. A motor-racing paddock seems always to hum to the tune of repeated stories and half-remembered anecdotes, for all of the great motor-racing circuits are rich in remembrances of the races and men who have come their way before. The names of most of Silverstone's corners are unchanged from the circuit's earliest days and still carry the sepia tinge of a former era – Woodcote, the jinxing corner leading on to the straight; the Abbey curve that links the two halves of the circuit; the demanding Copse, always inviting you to go a little faster, and Stowe, the right-hander named after the public school that stands in the near distance. All of them are names that appeared on the circuit's original plans and all of them will certainly be there for as long as it remains in use.

It is the same in Monaco, where the circuit's layout has barely changed in seventy years of racing, or Spa-Francorchamps, the swooping, wonderful home of the Belgian Grand Prix, whose quicksilver corners have survived years of safety work and aesthetic tinkling. At Monza, the steep brick banking that once threatened ever-greater risks has now fallen into disuse and disrepair, but its crumbling walls are scaled each year by curious supporters, hunting for an echo of the past.

The sentimentality that causes those fans to scale the crumbling Monza banking is one of a cluster of basic emotions that keep Formula One alive. There is curiosity, aggression, fear and a healthy smattering of greed, all of them co-existing uneasily.

Curiosity though is the most important, for without that single sensation motor racing would be redundant. We want to know more than simply who won a race and by what margin.

What advantage did his car offer him? How did he get past an opponent? How sophisticated is the machinery he uses? Which drivers are friends, and do they help each other? From every corner a new question springs up.

Motor racing does not have the obviousness of football or boxing, where the skills of players are clear for everyone to see. As observers, we know that David Beckham is highly talented because we can see him pass, trap and shoot a football with the precision of a sniper, but a racing driver is more difficult to assess, cocooned as he is inside a car, hidden from the world, his outward emotions masked by a crash helmet over his face. The crucial movements of hands and feet are covered by the shell of a car, almost impossible to make out.

As a result, it is no easy task to distinguish between a good driver and a mediocre one, for the margin is so narrow between the best and the worst that differences in style can be hard to perceive. Formula One cars perform to different levels, so outright speed could feasibly owe as much to the power of the engine as to the skill of the driver. Similarly, a car that slides through corners in spectacular fashion and then emerges in a blaze of photogenic spinning wheels will probably owe more to a driver's overindulgence than to outrageous talent.

At a fundamental level, the best drivers are the ones who make least mistakes, whichever car they might find themselves lumbered with. Even if they start a Formula One career behind the wheel of a car stranded at the back of the grid, hobbled by a poor engine or a cumbersome chassis, the finest racers go about their driving efficiently and relentlessly, taking as much as possible from the machinery while never pushing it too near to destruction.

In any team, the brightest talents outperform their opposite numbers, beating their team-mates with faster qualifying times and better races. It is an internal battle of great significance, because the contest between team-mates can often prove decisive in a driver's career. When your opponent uses a similar machine defeat can no longer be explained away with the standard defence that the other guy had a better car, so it is little wonder that the timing sheets which emerge shortly after each practice session are scrutinized with an intensity that borders on paranoia. The best drivers adapt quickly and, like the young Michael Schumacher, exude a confidence that motivates and solidifies their team. It took Schumacher only a year to impose his character so strongly on his new colleagues at Benetton that he, rather than the car, became their focus, and they worked to whatever agenda he chose to set.

Now, confident, successful and proven, Schumacher embodies the entire future of the sport; its new order of tactics, of ethics and of money-drenched political intrigue. Not only is he a driver of rare natural talent, but he is as commercially minded as a weathered businessman, forceful in his demands and conscious of the need to smile for cameras and stimulate the interest of the world's press. If ever a man has come to personify his sport, then it is this young German.

Schumacher is one of those rare drivers whose ability is obvious even to those with little technical knowledge of racing Since his days as a kart racer, he has developed into a potent combination of predator and opportunist, a driver who harries his rivals into mistakes and then takes advantage instinctively. He pushes rules to the limit, and encourages those around him to do the same, throwing into question the traditional boundaries of ethics and morality that have clung to Formula One for years.

In 1994, the year of his first world title, Schumacher came to the final grand prix, held in Adelaide, leading the championship by a single point from Damon Hill, his only challenger. In the ensuing race, the pair were together at the front when Schumacher made a mistake, clipping a wall as he rounded a curve, and badly damaging his car. As Hill appeared behind him, moving to one side to overtake the stricken Benetton, Schumacher moved into his  path, a seemingly deliberate act of last-ditch desperation, and the pair collided, both cars suffering enough damage to force them out of the race. Amid cries of foul play, Schumacher was crowned champion

He retained the title a year later and then moved to Ferrari, the sport's most famous driver taking a seat in its most famous team. A year after that, he tried his trick again when, in another last-race decider, he attempted to barge Jacques Villeneuve off the track with an ugly lunge as the Canadian driver moved to pass him. This time, though, it was Schumacher who came off second best, bouncing his car off Villeneuve's and into the clutches of a sand-trap that seized his wheels and bogged the Ferrari down into helpless retirement. Villeneuve, his car surprisingly undamaged by the collision, finished the race in third place and so won the title.

There have been other incidents, too, other times when Schumacher's driving has owed as much to intimidation as to his skill behind the wheel. In another era, this would have been frowned upon, his attitude of apparent disdain for opponents considered unacceptable, but Schumacher is as near to untouchable now as any driver in Formula One's history, hero-worshipped as much by the sport as by those who watch it.

He represents a potent advertisement for motor racing, a Ferrari driver of sublime skill who has a uniquely combative attitude to his racing. He will take exactly the same sort of liberties for which other drivers are castigated, but Schumacher has that crucial defence of being acknowledged as the best in the field, the man the world wants to watch. As long as people tune in to watch motor racing because of Michael Schumacher, then he will be the sport's most pandered cash cow, and in a sport where money counts above all else, his global appeal will always provide him with the equivalent of a royal pardon.

Ten years ago, when motor racing could boast such strong-minded men as Ayrton Senna, Alain Prost, Nigel Mansell and Nelson Piquet among its number, drivers who were happy to play up to a television camera or speak their mind to a cluster of newspaper journalists, the sport was awash with the sort of controversy and rancorous rivalry that delights any promoter, and particularly one as powerful as Bernie Ecclestone. Since the death of Senna in 1994, though, Formula One has become a much more settled environment, one that has come perilously close to being polite, and Ecclestone has shuddered.

Schumacher is the ace in his pack. At the start of the 1998 season, when it seemed the McLaren team were about to dominate the year's events, Schumacher produced one of his classic pieces of opportunism, exploiting a slight mistake by David Coulthard, the McLaren driver leading the Argentine Grand Prix, to force his way past and almost knock Coulthard off the road in the process. An hour and a half later, the Ferrari won the race.

Coulthard was outraged for it seemed to him that accepted standards of driving had been breached by the sheer aggression of Schumacher's manoeuvre, but his complaints were brushed aside. The trump card had appeared on the playing table, bringing controversy in its wake, and a television audience had woken up to a championship that had been in danger of seeming predictable. Ecclestone, and the sport's other promoters, were more interested in raising toasts to Schumacher than in castigating him for his bullishness.

Controversy and combativeness are the traits that television loves, and the extent to which Formula One has been transformed into a small-screen spectacle cannot be overestimated. Global viewing figures are bandied about like confetti at a wedding, suggesting that just about everybody in the world watches grand-prix racing at some point, but even if those statistics are greeted with justifiable scepticism by many who hear them, the sport's success in marketing itself is beyond doubt. Only the Olympics and the football World Cup draw more viewers and, as Formula One's administrators enjoy pointing out, they take place only once every four years.

Motor racing at the highest level offers the home viewer a blend of emotion, intrigue and competition wrapped up in easily consumed chunks – part sport, part business and part open warfare. It pushes its participants to the extremes of endurance, subjecting them to gravitational forces that would knock out an untrained driver and demanding a level of fitness to match that of a marathon runner.

As a spectacle, it appeals to an audience on several levels. There is the Saturday morning matinée excitement of watching a tense car race with the lurking risk of a driver crashing and the intrigue of trying to work out the tactical plans at work. Increasingly, television offers the chance for spectators to place themselves inside the car and imagine the thoughts of each driver, for in-board cameras, robust and smoothly efficient, create the illusion that your armchair has been moved to the centre of the cockpit, throwing you into the heart of the sport.

Road safety statistics show that most people have an inflated sense of their own driving ability, the average person is scarcely aware of dangers on the road or even the capabilities of their own car. But the ease with which racers appear to do

their job, as seen by those in-board cameras, adds to the fallacy that racing is a straightforward task.

Deceptively easy. It could be this sport's catchphrase, its mission statement to the public who watch so eagerly, and the sponsors who pour money into the Formula One coffers with just as much relish. Everything is planned to the last detail from the lavish facilities laid on to comfort guests to the shining gleam of each car, buffed up like a Rolls-Royce coming out of the showroom. The races start precisely on time and the parade of flags, each carried by a hand-picked model, is choreographed with the care of a dance troupe.

Deceptively easy, too, is the arrival of the motor-racing circus in each of the cities it visits. Around Europe, the teams transport themselves in articulated lorries painted in the sponsors' colours, yet when the races are further afield, and an increasing number of them are, the materials go by air, packaged up in jumbo jets that fly ton upon ton of parts and spares around the globe. At the other end, the crates are unloaded, put on lorries and delivered to the race circuit where, like an army of soldier ants, the mechanics get to work, building the dream.

There are five days to a grand prix, five days in which the sport puts down its roots, delivers its entertainment and then, like Mr Barnum's big top, disappears into the twilight. Formula One becomes the focal point for a region, dominating its life, its spectators and its television chat shows. In return, the race turns the eyes of the world on to the country and imbues it with the received glamour of Formula One racing. A weekend of racing in exchange for a place in the television sun.

The weekend begins on a Thursday morning, when mechanics affiliated to each team arrive at the circuit. Cars do not take to the track until the following morning, but the fastidious nature of Formula One means there is always preparatory work to be done.

Each car is tended to by mechanics who have their own areas of expertise. A couple will specialize in the rear of the machine, others in the front. One will concern himself with the peculiarities of the gearbox while another works on the suspension. They work assiduously to the

rhythm of pop music, a booming beat that changes in content, but not volume, from garage to garage.

Collectively, the mechanics are responsible for ensuring that the car works as well as possible. Like the drivers themselves, they are hostages to forces outside their control, for no part can be entirely fail-safe under situations of enormous stress, and the mechanics can hardly be held responsible for mistakes in design or those committed by the driver.

On Friday, their work is put to the test for the first time during two one-hour long sessions when changes are made to each car, in search of what is known in the sport as the right

'set-up'. It is a woolly description, but universally used to refer to any adjustments made to parts of the car that affect its handling. Changing the brake balance, for instance, has a dramatic effect on the stability of a car as it enters a corner, while the tolerance of a shock absorber changes the car's ability to deal with the bumps present on every circuit.

The right set-up is crucial to a driver's performance, for a feeling of both physical comfort and confidence in the car's manoeuvrability is central to a driver's ability to race. After his first attempt at qualifying in the ill-behaved Arrows of 1997, Damon Hill memorably described the car as 'evil' and admitted he had little belief in its ability to go where instructed. From such seeds grow trepidation and uncertainty, and when those feelings creep in, then even the best driver is left all-but helpless. After all, would you put your life on the line in a car you were uncomfortable with?

Friday is the crucial precursor to the high-profile events of the following two days, yet it engenders an atmosphere of consideration rather than edge-of-the-seat nerves. From the outside, it appears uneventful and routine, entirely lacking the histrionics that inevitably creep in before the weekend is over, yet by the end of Friday's round of preparation, it is normally clear which drivers are well placed to qualify and race well, and which will struggle.

Not that outright speed is the definitive clue as to how

preparations are going, although certainly a driver who finishes both Friday sessions at the head of the timing sheet is generally pleased with the handling of his car. For others, though, it can be a smokescreen, an indication that a driver is putting everything into setting a fast time rather than considering the problems that lie within his car.

Like so much else in this sport, it is a question of looking beyond the times that appear on a screen. Cars carrying smaller amounts of fuel are lighter, so set quicker times. As do drivers who elect to use a fresh set of tyres for their runs, since new rubber clings to the road more effectively and allows cars to brake later into a corner and accelerate a little earlier on the exit. The fact that a Sauber is quicker than a Ferrari after Friday's first session usually provides little more than a thrill of achievement for the boys in the Sauber garage, and even they know that the positions are likely to be reversed when the serious business gets under way.

For the fans, though, the intricacies are of little importance. Only two countries – Germany and Italy – host more than one grand prix per year, so for most spectators, sitting in grandstands or craning their necks from a grass bank, Friday offers the year's first opportunity to study a Formula One car at close quarters. From 11 a.m., when the first car takes to the track, there is a sense of that expectation being gradually fulfilled, with cheers and applause greeting the most famous names as they appear for the first time. By 2 p.m., the end of the second period of action, most appetites have been sated.

There are always unanswered questions, of course, and there is time for more testing on Saturday morning when the circuit is again opened up for the teams to tinker with their set-

up a little more. Saturday, though, is about something more than supposition and speculation, it is the day when the race grid is decided. Over the course of an hour-long qualifying session, and after a snatched lunch, each driver is assigned twelve laps to try to set the fastest lap time possible.

In order to minimize the weight of the car, and to allow the driver to make last-minute changes to the set-up, those twelve laps are usually divided up into four groups of three – one to speed up, one to set a fast time, and then one to return to the pits. He has, in effect, four attempts to set the best time of the day, four attempts to win the right to start a race from the pole position mark at the front of the grid.

Most drivers play conservatively with their opening lap in order to have one decent time in the bank. After that, it is a game of brinkmanship, each affecting an appearance of self-conscious nonchalance and waiting to see what his rivals will do. Like latter-day prize fighters, they soak up each blow and try to hit back harder.

While the races themselves reward tactical acumen and consistency, qualifying is about the ability to summon speed. Fast drivers do not always make great drivers, but they do make great qualifiers. Ayrton Senna did not have the racecraft of his fierce rival, Alain Prost, which is why Prost won more races and championships. Senna, though, had the gift of outright speed, a natural sensitivity to his car mixed with shots of bravery, self-confidence and loosely reined-in aggression. In 161 grands prix, he qualified in pole position 65 times, almost twice as many as any other driver in the sport's history.

If Saturday afternoon is about a starburst of adrenaline and energy, then the rest of the day is about anticipation. For drivers as much as spectators, there is a curiosity and, for those who feel they have a chance of winning, a sense of nervousness. Behind the familiar expressions of quiet confidence, every driver approaches a grand prix morning with a sense of intrigued excitement.

For the likely winners, there is the burden of living up to the expectation of team and fans. Even for the also-rans, there is the chance that fate will suddenly turn its favour and a car will emerge from the pack to win.

In 1996, Olivier Panis, driving the justifiably unfancied Ligier, took advantage of an extraordinary series of retirements among his fellow drivers and won the Monaco Grand Prix, the most celebrated race in the world. Two decades previously, Vittorio Brambilla won the Italian Grand Prix at Monza, the only time in his career that he was to finish a Formula One race in the top three, and was so excited that as he waved to the crowd on his slowing-down lap, he crashed his car into a barrier. Accidents are part of the sport, and Brambilla's luck was to crash when the race had finished. All it takes is a spin at the first corner, and a driver's weekend will be over just a few moments into a race, rendering useless those long hours of preparation by his team. In qualifying or practice sessions, he can climb into a spare car or wait for his to be repaired, but errors during a grand prix do not earn such a reprieve.

For men who are usually so full of self-confidence, the walk back to a pit garage after an early crash can be both long and embarrassing, but for every driver who retires from the race there will be lengthy meetings in which problems are studied, solutions devised and recriminations made. Only rarely can the whims of bad luck take all the blame.

For the winner, the champagne-drenched jubilation is obvious, and there will be others sharing the joy – stragglers picking up a first point of the season or a lowly team who surprised themselves by getting a car to the chequered flag. In the paddock after a race, the clash of emotions is obvious, as celebratory party tapes boom out from one motorhome while another team packs up solemnly. It is impossible to escape the smiles of those who have tasted victory, who have waved their delight to fans and received an ovation of applause in return.

And then, as abruptly as it arrived, the trappings of the sport disappear again. On Sunday night and in to the early hours of Monday morning, the trucks are packed up ready to return to the team's factory where the cars can be stripped down, repaired and then prepared once more for a grand prix.

Behind them, the teams leave an empty paddock and the debris of a weekend's racing, the pieces of tape, the empty boxes and the discarded minutiae of a sport that is high in consumption. This, then, is the fifth day, when the cleaners arrive and the fans return in search of keepsakes, when the track relaxes after its pounding and the streets return to normal. The day when the people of Monaco, Imola, Monza or Silverstone reclaim their towns and resume their lives free from the scrutiny of the world's cameras.

Five days, and each is as different in character as the drivers who fling themselves along straights and around corners at speeds the rest of us can barely comprehend. Within the ranks of a sport and its fans dwell confidence and ambition, humour, warmth and companionship, but the façades of pure commercialism and sporting battle can blind us to all else.

The trick in Formula One is to scratch the surface a little deeper, to look for the signs of humanity on the circuit and the grass banks, in the paddock and at the souvenir stands. To look at the thousands of people digging themselves beds from a hillside at Imola, or the millionaires peering from the hotel rooms in Monaco, woken by the sound of Sunday morning's warm-up session, or even at the smiling Finn who has just been crowned world champion.

By rights, a world that is more environmentally aware than ever before should reject Formula One's petrol-driven consumerism, but it never will. The appeal of whining engines and talented racers is too potent to ignore, and the history and heritage draws us back time after time. However much it may be covered in tobacco sponsors' stickers, or drenched in rain and mud, or obscured by money and politics, Formula One has a heart that is kept fresh by the enthusiasm of its world. As long as people keep watching, the heart will beat as strongly as ever.

Thursday

For all the noise and clamour, motor racing demands an element of contemplation from its participants and even, perhaps, from its supporters. Without any cars to disturb the peace of Thursday morning in Imola, two fans doze at the gate, pondering the events that will unfold over the coming days, enjoying the sun, absorbing the moment.

The Rivazza corner at Imola is a challenge for drivers who round it on the way to the finishing line, but the corner holds more interest as the favoured vantage point for thousands of spectators who make impromptu camps on the hillside and then spend days living in them. By the end of the weekend the waving grass will have been worn away, and only mud and litter will remain. For the moment, though, the emphasis is on finding the right spot to set up home.

At the point where Ayrton Senna's life came to an end a shrine has grown up and fans come to remember their favourite driver in peace. As motor racing lost its finest competitor so it rediscovered a sense of mortality, for Senna's death, and that of Roland Ratzenberger the previous day, were the first for many years. On the back of every entrance ticket to a Grand Prix are the words 'motor racing is dangerous', a legal warning, but it took the death of a champion to bring home the point to a generation brought up to feel untouchable.

If cleanliness is next to Godliness then there can be no sport nearer to the heavens than Formula One. Wherever you look in the paddock, truck windscreens shine like diamonds, litter is swept away and the smears of oil are swiftly wiped away from racing cars. The days when motor racing was fuelled by sweat and grease have long since gone and the corporate image of today's racers is clean-cut with clean hands.

A long, dusty drive from Austria to Imola with a few hundred litres of beer in the back of a motorhome and five days of racing and communal relaxing in front of them. For these fans, tired from their journey but buoyed up with enthusiasm for the annual jaunt to the races in Italy, the drinking is about to start early . . .

. . . and so is the singing. Who needs a microphone when there's a stick handy and your voice carries for miles?

In the pit lane the preparations are scrupulous. On Thursday, when no cars are allowed to take to the track, the machinery is readied carefully for the days ahead, examined by teams, scrutinized by officials and tended to by mechanics with the care of maternity nurses. Behind them, the vast empty stands of the Hockenheim circuit in Germany impose their own sense of urgency, a reminder that the fans will soon be arriving.

Hundreds of tyres are used by Formula One's teams at every race; thousands every year. Like the parts of a car, they have to be checked repeatedly and looked after with care, for tyres offer the driver his only contact with the earth while travelling at speeds that reach above 200 miles per hour.

Check, check and check again. By the time a car runs for the first time, it has been taken apart and rebuilt several times, all in the hunt for the slightest problems that may lurk within. The various parts are subjected to such extreme pressures that even the smallest mistake will have ramifications that will be both rapid and damaging. Cars regularly retire from races with mechanical failures that can be traced back to a component costing just a few pence but which has been wrongly fitted.

New drivers rarely find themselves overwhelmed by acceleration but are frequently staggered by the ability of a Formula One car's brakes. In the Williams pit they are examined and prepared for the action that lies ahead, during which the brakes will reach temperatures running into hundreds of degrees centigrade.

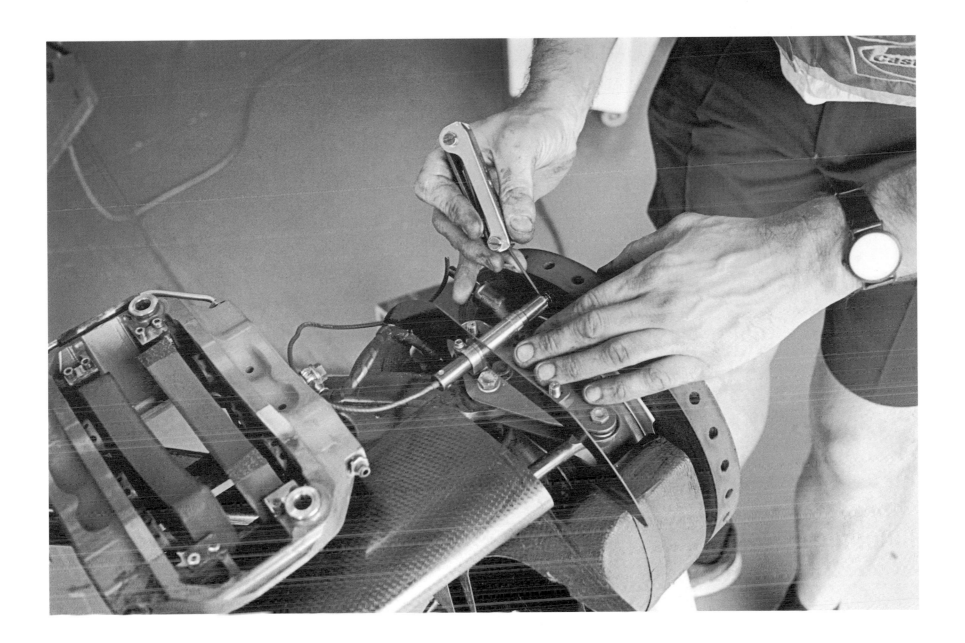

A driver's greatest rival is his team-mate, who provides the benchmark that he must strive to beat. Jacques Villeneuve and Heinz-Harald Frentzen, Williams' drivers in 1998, lay out their battle uniforms – helmet, gloves, earplugs – and ready themselves for the conflict ahead of them. For them Thursday is also a day of preparation, of acquainting themselves again with a circuit, thinking through its particular challenges and composing both body and mind for the demands of speed and competition.

It is glamour that first attracts sponsors to Formula One with its echoes of heroism, drama and bravado, and it is glamour that these sponsors then try to inject into the sport through their billboards and glossy magazine advertisements. In Melbourne, a fashion model drapes herself around a set of tyres, trying her best to make them look alluring and seductive.

Even as he reads mail in an office deep within Argentina's Buenos Aires circuit, Jacques Villeneuve is a public figure under public scrutiny, prey to the battery of cameras that shadow the move of every driver. Meanwhile, outside Hockenheim's main gates, thousands of eyes examine the faces of each person to drive past, eager to find the next celebrity who will sign books and shake hands. Those not judged interesting receive an abrupt cold shoulder from all around, leaving a lingering feeling of guilt for disappointing so many people with anonymity.

At midnight, a Monaco shopkeeper lays out a collection of T-shirts that he has prepared specially to sell at the race. His normal line of trade has been suspended for the weekend in order to make way for souvenirs, and he diligently folds each shirt into a smart parcel, ready to be sold at a hefty profit. In Monaco, after all, there is very little for the bargain-hunters.

Friday

Of all the motor-racing circuits in the world, only Monaco has an immovable place In the sport's inconstant heart, a result of its historical connections and singular layout, drawn over public roads that pass a procession of landmarks. In the early hours of Friday morning, while most of the principality sleeps, finishing touches are made to the track and the occasional car passes by on streets that are still open to the public. The anticipation is growing.

At every Grand Prix, spectators can buy a ticket which allows them to enter the pit lane at certain, strictly controlled, times for a wander around. In Silverstone, a father takes his son to stand on the wall from which signals are passed during a race, while behind them crowds amass in front of each team's garage. Ferrari, of course, provide the biggest draw.

Wheels within wheels, wherever you look.

Movement. As Silverstone opens itself to another pit-lane walkabout, fans stroll past the middle-ranking cars in search of the McLarens, Ferraris and Williams garages that lie just beyond. Behind those doors, Jacques Villeneuve walks away from his car to talk to engineers and strategists. Around him, mechanics get ready to tend to the car and to set it up for the next session.

When tiredness strikes it can be hard to resist. In Imola, as the crowd continues to pour into the circuit, one fan catches up on lost sleep as he basks in the early-morning sun.

A good view is a precious asset for the motor-racing fans who choose to come and see their sport in the flesh. Races attract many tens of thousands of spectators, each of them anxious to see the action unfold, and some fans plan their viewing with the dedication of a military coup. A makeshift grandstand, standing between two mobile homes, is the prize for those with the foresight to bring scaffolding poles with them.

At the Rivazza corner the grass is wearing thin and the camping spots are running out. Fans carve huge steps out of the hillside to give themselves a smooth bench upon which to watch and then sleep, but building the benches takes time, energy and, in the case of one fan, a large pickaxe. Almost without exception, the devotees who come to watch in this way support the red of Ferrari with their flags and banners, and as Friday's action continues so too does the queue of fans who climb the steps to Rivazza, and prepare to make their homes in the hill.

If glamour is part of motor racing's culture then publicity is its partner. Formula One's sponsors want to see their cars on as many screens and newspaper pages as possible, so they demand publicity stunts from their teams in the lull of a Friday afternoon. Incongruous in the workshop of the Jordan team, model Emma Noble, dressed to the whims of the team's principal sponsor, smiles for the cameras.

Away from the track, though, the glamour is less evident and the sport's soul is harder but less fickle. The campsites dotted around Silverstone are prey to muddy flooding when rain starts to fall, as it invariably does at some point, yet resilience is part of the supporter's experience. Their flags show their loyalties; T-shirts under grey skies suggest a streak of optimism that suits motor racing to its core.

Motor racing is still a sport best watched in the sun on a clear afternoon. As drivers fine-tune their cars at Imola, the light glints off a fan's travelling home, parked in pride of place a few yards from the track.

Others, of course, prefer a more dramatic seat from which to watch the practice sessions unfold. A Ferrari follower takes to his eyric, looking down on the scarlet machines as they fly past below.

Stand in the middle of the pit lane and you can see two worlds within one sport. To your left, the teams who live on hope and expectation; to the right, those who arrive with a realistic chance of winning the race. As the mechanics from Prost and Jordan tend to their cars, each team is aware of their place in the pecking order, and it is Prost who are slipping down.

The competitive Jacques Villeneuve throws down the gauntlet.

Friday afternoon, and the cars have run for one hour and have another hour to go. In the interval, they are stripped down, changes are made to the various parts and then the cars are rebuilt, once more to be pushed to their limits. Wheels come on and off the car as a matter of routine, dislodged and then re-attached by airguns that lie on the floor of every pit garage and then scream into action.

There is beauty in Formula One, but it is rarely obvious. Under the skin of a racing car sits an exhaust system that has to be sculpted by hand and tended to with devotion. None of the pipes must touch and each must be precisely the same length, yet from such cold demands come swooping pieces of industrial architecture.

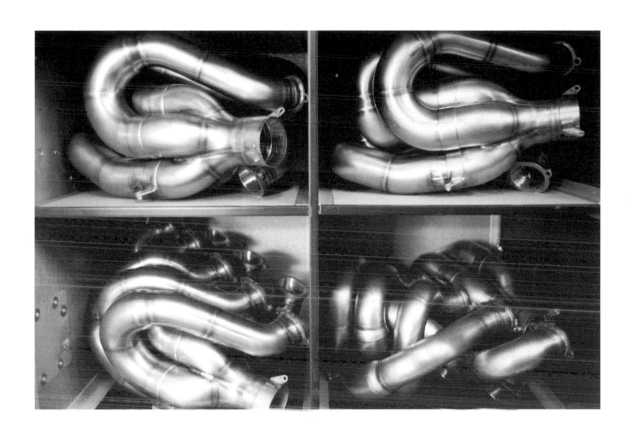

Even above the sensations that run through a driver's body, there is only one way to gauge a car's performance, and that is by looking at the lap-times that each records. A good run on Friday afternoon could prove the springboard for a strong race performance, and there is pride and confidence to be gained in setting the fastest time. Ralf Schumacher studies the television monitors with their screens full of data that marks his progress.

A few garages away from his brother, Michael Schumacher also ponders, looking for his own time and also those of his competitors. If they are quicker he wants to know why, and how he can close the gap. If Schumacher is the fastest, then he will still push his team to try ever harder, motivating them with the promise of victory. The skills of the greatest drivers are never confined to their ability behind the steering wheel.

The ability of a driver to translate his experiences and problems with a car into words has a direct bearing on what changes the team make to the machinery. Heinz-Harald Frentzen, like many others, mimics the movements of his hands on the steering wheel, recalling the events of each lap and passing on advice to the listening Williams engineers. As long as there is time to make a change then it will be done.

The driver is the most famous figure in any racing team, but he would be foolish to assume an air of self-importance in front of the very people who build and tend to his car. Alexander Wurz, a young Austrian in the early years of his career, returns to the pits at the end of his practice session to share a joke with his colleagues from the Benetton team.

Once the cars have stopped pounding round the track and the engines have been turned off a silence slowly eases itself over the world's noisiest sport. The machines that had roared are now pushed to one side and slowly taken apart, propped up on stands like fighter planes being prepared for battle while every part is examined. Just as the engine is checked for faults and its oil routinely changed, so the smallest gearcogs are tested out, spun by a mechanic with the ease of a child whirling a top.

Even for those whom we might imagine have seen it all before, motor racing continues to hold an allure that transcends simple business acumen. Frank Williams, stimulated by the scent of competition even on a Friday when the opposition comes only from the clock, watches his mechanics as they tend to the cars that carry his name.

For Formula One the price of success has been a siege mentality at the circuit, for the sport generates so much attention that it is forced to isolate its heart, protecting the paddock in which the work is done. As the Friday crowd draws away, security men continue their patrols, looking for any unwanted intruders.

Saturday

For the fans who have waited all year to see Formula One cars in competitive action, Saturday morning marks the end of the pretence, and the beginning of real action. The promise of qualifying, where the grid and the favourites are established, draws in bigger crowds and offers more intense excitement. In Buenos Aires, these children have saved all year for the money to buy their entrance tickets. They do not expect to be disappointed.

Some of the competition on offer to fans dates from even further back than the mechanized warfare of Formula One. In Imola's shaded woodland, spectators while away the hours before qualifying begins by wagering money on the age-old game of Chase the Queen, a quieter sport than motor racing, but still highly profitable to the men who hold the right cards.

Anticipation is the impetus for watching motor racing, with its pronounced streaks of unpredictability, but it comes at a price for those who choose to watch their sport from the side
of the track. Whether in the campsite in Budapest or at a burger van at Silverstone, the lot
of a Formula One fan can slip far from the luxurious, and into the realms of the rudimentary.
As Saturday morning draws on so the rain begins to fall over Britain's grand-prix faithful.

Hockenheim's army of fans prepare for qualifying, united behind their totem, the Ferrari driver Michael Schumacher.

Most fans relate to drivers rather than teams, so it is Hill, Coulthard, Herbert and Irvine who draw the biggest support at Silverstone. Banners with each name are draped from grandstands and their appearances draw cheers that are muffled by the roar of the driver's engine. Even in the most global of sporting events the fire of nationalism is hard to put out, despite the best efforts of a Silverstone downpour.

Unlike football, where fans are watched closely for signs of trouble and alcohol is prohibited in most grounds, there have been very few instances of disruption among motor racing's vast crowds and drinking is seen as an acceptable part of the Formula One experience. In Hungary, the combination of sport, beer and a comfortable deckchair is too much for one fan to resist, while some of his countrymen pay the price for overdoing it. As qualifying begins and the engines start up noisily they continue to doze in the long, sun-warmed grass, undisturbed.

In the moments before the start of the hour-long qualifying session, drivers can do little more than wait in quiet anticipation of the challenge that lies ahead. They have refined the set-up of their cars, watched their rivals and chatted endlessly with engineers, but only now does the competitive weight fall entirely on to their shoulders, and those who can cope with the expectation will often be those who qualify at the front of the grid. Damon Hill watches the monitors in the Jordan team's garage and waits.

For some, the anticipation of pushing a car towards its mechanical limit in pursuit of a single flying lap can prove draining before a wheel has even turned. Others revel in such pressure, drawing strength from the anticipation of the crowd, the team, the rivals. In the Williams pit, Jacques Villeneuve chats to his engineers before zipping up his baggy overalls and pulling on his helmet. Only then, enclosed with just his thoughts for company, does the familiar smile disappear.

As the teams prepare for their Saturday finale there are other battles going on around the circuit. Drivers may rely on plates of pasta and vegetables for their lunchtime meal, but in Hungary, where vegetarianism and calorie-controlled diets are not pressing concerns, a cow is slowly cooked on a spit by a group of fans.

It could only be Italy. In Imola, the streets around the circuit are deserted as racing engines fire up and everybody has a vantage point to head to.

Because of the problems of reversing a Formula One car accurately, drivers simply stop their cars in front of the team garage and wait to be hauled back by mechanics. Jacques Villeneuve completes a lap in the qualifying session's opening moments and then returns to the refuge of the pits.

While the cars pass by outside, in the garage there is still time for the mechanics to look for answers. Books of data, readings from the internal workings of a car that are transmitted by computer link, have become motor racing's bible, but the solutions they promise are buried deep within columns of numbers and coloured graphs.

One of the most famous corners on a motor-racing circuit stands outside the front doors of the Loews Hotel in Monaco, a tight hairpin bend that bunches the cars together and threads them down a hill and towards the tunnel. It is a landmark of the track, even of the sport, and as the first qualifiers funnel past so the tension begins to build along the principality's stone walls and expensive grandstands. For the sunbathers who lounge by the pool that sits on top of the hotel, though, the atmosphere is more relaxed. Only the bark of racing engines from many floors below provides an intrusive hint that Formula One has come to town.

In Monaco there is a premium placed on securing a strong qualifying position, for the narrow, twisty circuit renders overtaking all but impossible during the race and those who start low down on the grid will struggle to score any points. Jacques Villeneuve cuts a corner by the harbour to search for greater speed but, as he ponders the timing sheets, it is clear that the effort is not being rewarded. The margin between elation and frustration can be narrow.

Rooms with a view. Tickets for motor races are expensive, regardless of location, and the temptation for many is to sneak a view, however obscured it may be. In Imola a couple take a peek through the fence, with the tacit approval of a lurking steward, while a grille on Monaco's steepling hillside offers the briefest of glimpses of the cars below.

Over the course of the hour-long qualifying session, an array of changes are made to each car, rapid fixes to deal with weather conditions and a track that offers varying levels of grip to the drivers. Formula One machinery is designed to be accessible, disassembling quickly and then fitting back together with the ease of a fountain pen sliding into its lid, so putting the front wing back on to this Williams car is the matter of a moment.

Around the streets of Monaco, Jacques Villeneuve continues his quest for the perfect lap and a higher place on the grid. The circuit is the slowest on the sport's annual calendar and, for a charger such as Villeneuve, it offers a test of patience as much as outright speed. Where he would accelerate hard out of corners on other circuits, he must be prudent in Monte Carlo.

Tension in the grandstands; tension in the pits. At Ferrari, all eyes are
on the timing screens that show the progress of their two drivers,
Eddie Irvine and Michael Schumacher, as they chase a fast lap time.

Like many drivers, Alexander Wurz chooses to take time away from his car to collect his thoughts and prepare for the rush of adrenaline that awaits him. Only when he is ready to go does Wurz pull on his flameproof balaclava and helmet, symbols of his readiness to enter the battle. Meanwhile, In Hockenheim's mammoth grandstands spectators watch agog and, like a cinema audience, peer round a late arrival as he searches for a seat.

Qualifying is over, and the tension eases from the watching fans with a sigh, a smile and a wave of the flag. On the Rivazza hillside, it is the culmination of hours of anticipation, for the scene has been set for the following day's race and already the conversation is concerned only with predicting the winner. At the foot of the hill, spectators climb to the exit or wander at the base of the concrete steps surrounded by the detritus of a day's sport.

For those who have stayed on the hillside, now terribly worn by the twin ravages of the campers' pickaxes and the shoes of so many spectators, the afternoon draws into evening. There is little to watch on the track any more, so while some read and talk, others drink and party, sounding air horns and huddling around a transistor radio to listen to a football match. Amid so much bustle some benefit from their overwhelming weariness and bide their time in sleep, slumbering under Imola's dying sun.

In the land of earth beds, the man with the lilo will
be king. Especially when he's wearing a Ferrari cap.

Imola has been blessed with good weather and the Rivazza hill is still warm enough for T-shirts as afternoon turns to evening. Dinner for these fans is a couple of bowls of pasta, brought to the event with them and cooked over an ingeniously small stove. To their side, work continues on a new and ambitious project as new arrivals prepare one of the largest earth bunks of the weekend. They drink as they go, smiling and singing to keep up spirits, and the empty bottles find a home as foundations to their communal home. They will not finish work until both darkness and the temperature have fallen.

If the empty track gives the impression that Formula One has finished its work, then it is a misguided one. In motorhomes parked in the paddock, drivers and engineers discuss their achievements, their successes and failures, and ponder strategies for the race that lies ahead. Behind them, in the garage, as much attention goes into preparing the cars for the final, and most significant, challenge.

By Sunday morning, every part will have been stripped down, examined, repaired, reassembled and cleaned. By this stage of the weekend, mechanics have routinely gone short of sleep, relaxation and food, yet their job is more vocation than profession and they are little prone to dissolving into dissatisfaction. However uncomfortable the work and its conditions may be, jobs in the sport's team garages are prized like diamonds.

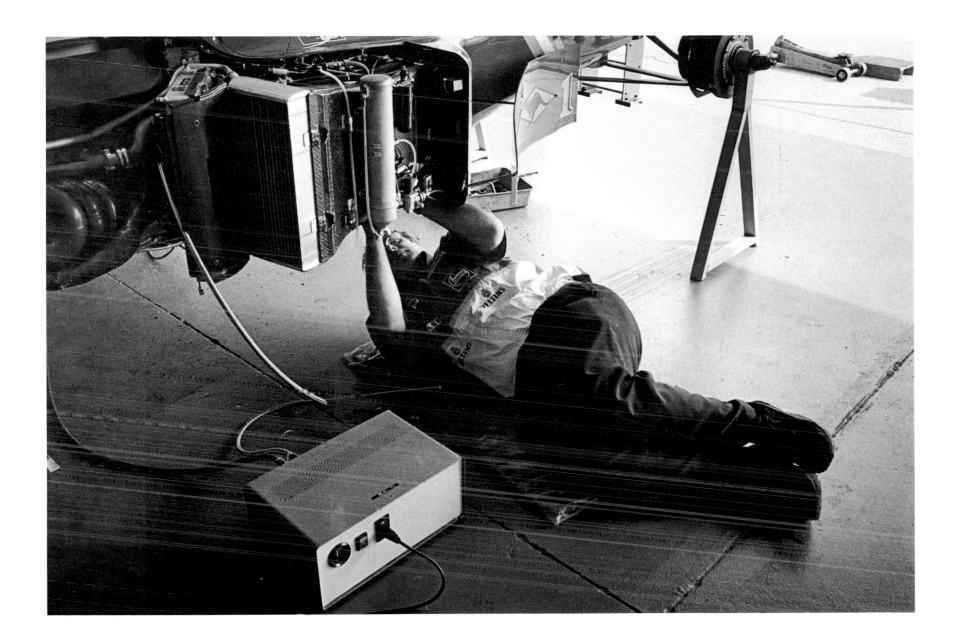

For some fans, the price of support can be painful. In Hockenheim, paramedics tend to a supporter who toppled from a low bridge as he led the cheering for Michael Schumacher. His last view of the circuit this year will be of the Ferrari flags imploring his favourite driver to live up to the anticipation of his home crowd.

As darkness falls, the pit lane still beats to the noise that spills from every garage, for the prerogative to play loud music is one that the mechanics will never be asked to give up. Even the best-prepared teams can find themselves working long into the night after qualifying, preparing for race days, and stories abound of mechanics who spent Saturday night working on a car, repairing damage and fitting new parts, checking machinery and then checking again. The race looms and, more than ever, they cannot afford to make mistakes.

Sunday

However experienced a driver may be he must attend a briefing on Sunday morning to be reminded of the sport's rules and regulations. The meeting often turns into an unofficial forum for debate between the competitors, the one time during a weekend when they are all gathered together to talk over problems. In Hungary, it is the McLaren drivers David Coulthard and Mika Hakkinen who arrive first but, symbolic of their season-long contest, Michael Schumacher is not far behind.

Like sports fishermen who wait hours for the next big fish, Hungary's autograph hunters
are prepared to bide their time until a major star appears. For Damon Hill, driving into
the circuit on the morning of the Grand Prix, there is the desire to please fans while also
keeping on the move. Should he stop in the middle of the crowd, his car will be engulfed
and Hill will be lucky to escape in time for the race, let alone the morning briefing.

In Monaco, where the living is a little easier, race day morning breaks with less commotion. The principality prides itself on tranquillity and order, so as one reveller sleeps off the previous night's excesses at the top of Monaco's famous hill a policeman conducts bustling traffic around the roads beneath. It will not be long before the same roads are cordoned off, ready to play host to Formula One's most famous event of the year.

The Paddock Club, a hub of corporate entertainment that overlooks the pits, charges many hundreds of pounds to cater for each guest over the course of a Grand Prix Sunday, providing gourmet food and a sweeping view. In the Williams team motorhome, however, sandwiches and a bottle of water provide a more straightforward sustenance for those whose work is about to be put to the test.

There are few sensations in sport to compare with the tension that lingers over a grid as the cars line up half an hour before a Formula One race on a Sunday afternoon. Each driver harbours his own hopes, tempered by his starting position, and each has his own way of preparing for the race. Mechanics and engineers, though, are suddenly helpless after so many hours and days of preparatory work, for they must now hand over the impetus to the man who sits in the cockpit. There is little more they can do but carry out final checks on the equipment and watch the time go by until the start of the race.

Blind love, suddenly uninterested in the race that is about to start.

In the Paddock Club, the well-heeled enter into the spirit while in the pit lane below their executive boxes airguns point to the typically meticulous preparations of each team. Spare wheels are placed on hand in case a car should return to the pits after the opening lap with a puncture, a result, perhaps, of the jostling that occurs at the first corner of every race. If ever a sport has adopted foresight as its watchword it is Formula One.

Just as boxing employs models to hold up message boards between rounds so motor racing clings to the glamour of pretty girls. Each is assigned a place on the grid, holding the home flag of the relevant driver and smiling cheerily for the procession of cameramen who wander past. On the morning of the race, the grid girls, as they have been known for many years, receive their instructions from a choreographer who likes them to practise and perfect a smile before taking up position.

The most prestigious role for any grid girl to attain is to mark out pole position, reserved for the leading driver in qualifying. As she stands and waits, smiling for the crowd, the quickest car nears the end of its warm up lap before winding through the crowded track and taking up its place at the front.

It is the moment when excitement shivers through a crowd, when the grid begins to clear of all but the cars and their drivers. There is no segregation within motor racing's supporters, and followers of Damon Hill are liable to find themselves standing shoulder-to-shoulder with those who wave flags for Michael Schumacher, yet all find unity in the trepidation that sweeps through hillsides and grandstands in those final moments.

Nerves, too, at the front of the grid, as those within a team worry about their driver and the car in which he sits. They worry that every part has been checked, that each part is correctly fitted, and that the race strategy is a good one that all understand. They worry to fill time and because the sensation rides on the back of the adrenaline that swirls round the grid like a tornado. And then the car is gone, and they are helpless to do any more.

Much of the length of the Hockenheim circuit is woody and unreachable for any but the most intrepid spectator. Instead, the great majority of the crowd sit in the arc of grandstands known as the stadium complex. From there fans watch the opening laps, waving German flags and wearing the red of Ferrari, urging on Schumacher. In 1994 he became the first German world champion, and the support he receives from his countrymen is overwhelming.

Mika Hakkinen, the eventual world champion, rides the kerbs in Budapest. Those who win Grands Prix blend aggression and outright speed with the control needed to keep a car on the manageable side of its limit.

At Rivazza the hillside is full to capacity as the race begins to unwind. From the bridge that passes over the track at its rear, where latecomers are reduced to watching through gaps in the wire, to the path at the top of the hill, there is no viewing position that has not been taken, reserved for hours before the first car took to the track.

Acclaim for a winner from one who watched him on his way.

Regardless of what countermeasures are put in place, there is invariably an invasion of the circuit in the minutes after the San Marino Grand Prix has taken place, and the Imola track suddenly plays home to hundreds, and then thousands, of *tifosi*. They clamber over the pit lane wall, searching for souvenirs and ripping down stickers and posters that are taken home as mementoes. It is not an outpouring of avarice or greed, but a desire to take home a tangible symbol of the events that have passed before them.

On the podium, the top three finishers are presented with cups and bottles of champagne which, of course, are sprayed around in a theatrical flourish of apparent sporting camaraderie. The podium tableau, with its celebratory sense of fun, is too intoxicating for any driver to dismiss, a momentary link with the same emotions that have carried through any successful racing driver in the sport's champagne-soaked history.

Like the chilling peace that accompanies the end of a battle, silence drops over a racing circuit once the race is finished and the podium has been emptied. For those who have watched from the grandstands and hillsides, there is the choice between joining an escalating traffic jam or, like these supporters in Hungary, simply sitting back and reflecting upon the race they have just witnessed.

On the Rivazza hillside the crowds have gone and only a handful of people remain where thousands stood a few hours before. At its base, a smouldering fire burns among the tinder of discarded programmes, empty food boxes and discarded cigarette cartons, a rubbish heap left behind by a transient audience. They leave behind their excavations, collect belongings and disappear for another year.

Finally, as the Rivazza's natural amphitheatre begins to clear, a disparate group of scavengers emerges to search the debris for small pieces of food and metal. From one side comes an elderly man, smart in his suit, his eyes trawling the ground for a valuable glint, at the same time, on the other side of the path beaten down the spine of the hill, a mother searches while her son sits on the ground, bored and fidgeting. It is a depressing sight and one in stark contrast to the sporting opulence that motor racing so fervently celebrates.

Meanwhile, in Imola's pit lane the onrushing fans have found a sense of calm and revel in the sight of their sport going through its final motions. As the Williams mechanics pack up their team garage, spectators peer through the portholes in the door, observing each movement like visitors to an aquarium, delighting in the minutiae.

For the drivers, there is a constant round of interviews with every branch of the media. If it is not radio or television that beckon for an interview, there will be a newspaper reporter waiting with notebook in hand, always asking little more than a couple of questions, hoping for an exclusive story. With the sweat on his brow barely dry, Damon Hill takes on his first post-race press conference in Spain.

Rush hour at Imola as the crowd finds its way home from Rivazza. As gradual as the occupation of the hillside had been, its abandonment to the hands of others is over within the space of a few hours.

In the cramped confines of Monaco's obsolete pit lane, it is time to pack the lorries and set off home. By the end of the evening each garage will be empty and the Williams trucks will be well on their way back to the team's headquarters in England, packed as quickly and astutely as a Pickford's removal van by mechanics who have completed the same task so many times before that they are now expert at it. A few feet away, the circuit's main straight now throngs with people, strolling quietly and remembering the formula cars that had thundered past the point where they now amble away a sunny twilight.

Monday

Monday morning, but the Grand Prix that brought such spectacle in its wake still sits on the minds of those it touched. In Monaco, a waitress at the station hotel takes a moment's break to read the local newspaper and remember the race.

The swimming pool is one of Monaco's landmarks. It is built to Olympic standards and hosts international competitions, as well as providing a breathing space amid the crowded streets. The Grand Prix circuit passes by on all four sides, and the far end is dwarfed by an enormous grandstand, yet, less than a day since the race finished, life is returning to normal. The regular swimmers have returned to reclaim their pool, and only the temporary scaffolding and a forgotten banner bear witness to the previous day's bustle.

Mr Hill has left the building.

The race has gone, but the souvenirs remain. In Monaco, opposite the palace, the allure of Grand Prix racing's most famous location lingers throughout the year, so the trinkets of Formula One are always on sale.

It takes months of planning for Monaco's Grand Prix track to be set up, along with the grandstands, media facilities and medical back-up that are pivotal to modern motor racing. At dedicated venues, such as Silverstone or Hockenheim, there is far less preparatory work to be done, for the circuits are maintained all year, but Monaco is different. Every vestige of Formula One has to be put up and then, far more quickly than they appeared, they come down again, ready to be packed away in hidden storerooms to reappear the following year.

In Imola, where the rubbish still billows on the Rivazza hillside, the scavengers have returned for a second look. So many thousands of people stood, watched, slept and ate from this patch of land that their debris will take hours to search and, for those who support themselves in this way, it is time well spent.

It takes an army of people and equipment to broadcast a Grand Prix to the world, but when the cars have finished racing then it is time to start packing up to head off. The cameras go, the cranes come down and the coils of wire pile up, ready to move on with the circus.

All that is left are the memories and a few signs that the sport had come to town. The mark left by a racing tyre as it moved off will linger until the rain or a janitor's brush cleans it away and then, like the driver who left it behind, it will disappear. Next year, they will both be back, the cycle going round again.